Profits Over People

A Story of Tragedy and Corporate Malfeasance

Sherry Roe

This book is dedicated to my parents,
Thelma and Glenn "Jerry" Dukes, my brother Tony,
and all those who shared their stories in one form
or another; those who suffer from illnesses incurred
from working at the plant, those who died from
chemical exposure, and the families they leave behind.
This is for you.

ACKNOWLEDGMENTS

This book is a labor of love and wouldn't have been possible without the factory workers and retirees that were willing to be a voice for those who succumbed to illnesses from chemical exposure due to unsafe work conditions. Their accounting's will continue on to help those in the community who are sick or have succumbed to illnesses caused from illegal dumping by these factories. Together we can hold them accountable.

I owe a debt of deep gratitude to my lifetime friend and editor, Bridgett Sharp Siter. You have spent timeless hours over years and across the miles not only editing for this book but being a mentor, prayer warrior, counselor, sending me Scriptures and giving me the gentle nudge to keep writing when life got in the way.

I send big love to my sister, Glenda. I'm thankful for you everyday, for unselfishly taking on the sometimes difficult role of mothering me and for always keeping faith in me and pushing me to write "the book" for our parents. Although across the miles, too, you have always been quick and resourceful on the keyboard when I needed a fact verified, help researching, or just a listening ear.

I've always believed Jesus had his hand in my being able to complete this book and he places family and people in our lives at the right time, His time, to help Him help us. My love and thanks to Rick and Caroline Edwards, my sister, for their patience with me while finishing this and endless hours of editing, designing and bringing this labor of love into a book and to the shelf for you, my readers who have patiently waited as well.

TABLE OF CONTENTS

FOREWORD

Close your eyes and think of the state of Indiana. What do you see?

Do you see basketball legends, the Indy 500, or a colorful sunset across seemingly endless fields of corn and soy?

Indiana is indeed home to sports powerhouses, the so-called greatest spectacle in racing, and large-scale agriculture. It's also home to a much more industrial and much less idyllic legacy.

Small and midsize cities and towns throughout Indiana are experiencing alarming rates of cancer incidence and poverty. Many of these locales are places where multiple factories tied to regional, national, and global economies once produced goods and middle-class lifestyles for their residents. Many of these factories have long since closed – only their toxic legacies remain. Others are still operating, but with levels of reporting and oversight that some reasonable people find inadequate to protect public health.

As an environmental anthropologist who works in Indiana alongside environmental scientists and local residents on environmental contamination and human health, I first met Sherry Roe to discuss a round of environmental sampling. Sherry's reputation had long preceded her. By the time we first met, I had read about Sherry in newspapers, heard colleagues singing her praises, and was already following her Facebook group... Profits Over People. I am now honored to call her a colleague and friend.

In the pages that follow, Sherry Roe will take you on an intimate journey of hope, tragic loss, complicated grief, and growth. Based on over a decade of research, this book offers a compelling account of the complex interactions between exposures to toxic chemicals, the development of devastating diseases, and the challenges associated with holding corporations accountable for past and present toxic harms. Part intimate memoir, part detailed reportage, this book examines the literal death of the middle class in industrial cities and towns throughout the U.S. Midwest.

The struggles detailed in this book have historical roots, but they are far from history. At the time of writing, Indiana still leads the nation in the release of toxic chemicals per square mile and has the seventh highest rate of cancer mortality in the country. It is also home to over fifty Superfund sites – sites found to be so contaminated with hazardous wastes that they require a long-term response from the U.S. Environmental Protection Agency to minimize the impacts to residents from exposures to hazardous wastes. Some places like Kokomo, Indiana, an industrial town at the center of this book, have more than one.

This is a brave book, written by a brave woman.

I hope you'll enjoy reading it as much as I have.

Jennifer Lee Johnson
Associate Professor
Department of Community Sustainability
Michigan State University

PREFACE

This book includes a collection of stories shared with me by those who worked at factories under unsafe and unhealthy conditions – conditions that ultimately caused many to succumb to different forms of cancer, leukemia, various other blood disorders and lung disease. Though I've changed the names of those whose stories I share, sometimes at their request but mostly out of an abundance of caution, these are first-hand and eye-witness accounts from plant employees. I wrote this book to give voice to the victims of corporate malfeasance, greed, and negligence. It was a company that clearly valued profits over people.

CHAPTER 1

THE STORY OF MY PARENTS

A Beginning

Glenn Medford "Jerry" Dukes married Thelma Moore in 1957 in Kokomo, Indiana, where Jerry worked at Cabot Corp and Thelma waitressed at the Lighthouse Drive-In. Jerry adopted Thelma's son, Tony, and the couple soon added two more babies to the family before Thelma was hired on at the new Delco Plant 8 in 1961.

A two-income factory family in a small Midwestern, blue-collar town in the middle of the 20th century could expect to enjoy a comfortable, solidly middle-class lifestyle. They would own their own home and enjoy annual summer vacations. Life was mostly good, but the family experienced a period the older kids would later call "a really sad time" when Thelma suffered a miscarriage late into her fourth pregnancy. She went back to work at Delco and was later able to successfully deliver another baby, this one a healthy baby girl, in 1966.

That baby girl was me, Sherry Lynn Dukes Roe, and this is my story as much as it is their's.

Jerry, Thelma, and Tony at 6 months old
on their wedding day

I am the youngest of Jerry and Thelma's four children. My older siblings and my younger brother, Shane, and adopted sister Caroline,

Thelma Dukes, second on the left, commemorating the 50 millionth car radio in 1966. I was 6 months old.

who were born to Dad and his second wife, Carolyn, can vouch for the facts, but not for my memories or my perspective. We each suffered the loss of our parents/dad in different ways, at different points in our lives, with unique challenges.

After my birth, life was busy and really good for three more years, until Mom began to suffer irregular menstrual cycles, dizziness, and severe stomach pain in 1968, seven years after starting work in the factory. The doctor discovered multiple tumors throughout her reproductive system and Mom underwent a radical hysterectomy at the age of 29. The ordeal sent her into an emotional tailspin, but with four children between them, Mom and Dad made peace with the finality of the surgery and she went back to work soon after.

Thelma on the right with her sister, Reba

Ironically, Mom urged Dad to leave Cabot for fear the foundry was unsafe and unhealthy. In 1972, he was hired on at Delco. Soon after, Mom found a lump in her breast and was diagnosed with carcinoma; her body was riddled with cancer. She underwent a double mastectomy, started an experimental chemotherapy and radiation plan, and went back to work with the understanding that her condition was terminal. She hoped the treatments would buy her some time with her family. Perhaps it did; Mom enjoyed two more years with us before succumbing to cancer on a hot Saturday morning in July of 1974. She was 36 years old. The cause of death was breast cancer.

I was 8 years old when mom died, so my memories of her are few and faded. I grieved as I grew up and longed to remember the sound of her voice and the feel of her touch. But I never forgot her work ethic. Mom worked in the factory right up until two days before her death.

She was a hard worker and a dedicated employee, but her work was a means to an end. Her greatest joy was her family, and she fought hard for her life out of a desire to see her children grown. If she ever suspected her work at Delco was causing her cancer, she didn't tell anyone. Until we made the connection, my sister and I lived with the fear that we were genetically predisposed to breast cancer.

Ten years ago, while combing through papers after my father's death, I discovered my mother's death record and papers that revealed that Mom, at the time of her death, was one of 12 women under the age of 40 employed in Plant 8 who died of breast cancer.

Mom

Mom was born August 7, 1937 in Celina, Tennessee, to Fred and Benzie Moore. She was born into poverty. Mom would eventually be sent to Indiana with some of her siblings to be raised by her aunt and uncle because her parents couldn't afford to feed all the children. Her aunt and uncle were loving people, but I couldn't imagine being separated from

Thelma, front row to left in floral print dress with her siblings and mother, Benzie, before she was sent to Indiana to live with her Aunt and Uncle

15

the rest of your family at such a young age. Of course, I know the pain of being separated from my mom at a young age. I only have a few memories of her, those that I have aren't the best, meaning they involved her being sick.

I do remember once being very sick myself with the flu, and mom slept with me all night. I didn't realize until I was an adult what a sacrifice that was. She was getting chemotherapy and contracting the flu could have killed her. She made lots of sacrifices; that's what mothers do. She was terminally ill, and chemotherapy and radiation were experimental back then. Grandma said she did it hoping to buy some more time with me, her youngest. She worried that I wouldn't remember her.

My Mother Thelma's grave in Sharpsville, Indiana

I remember Mom lining us kids up and telling us she was going to go to be with Jesus. We were to behave like perfect ladies and gentlemen at her funeral and absolutely no crying. We weren't to go to the cemetery because it would just make us sad, and she wouldn't be there anyway.

My paternal grandma said Mom left her a list of wishes for all us kids. My mom was Catholic and she told grandma to make sure I went to the Baptist church with her "because Catholics got away with too much." I always found that humorous, but you can be sure I spent every Sunday morning next to grandma in the pew at her Southern Baptist church.

I sometimes asked Dad to "tell me about Mom." He always got tears in eyes and said, "I just can't."

Shamefully, I think I blocked a lot of memories of Mom, because I associated them with her death. After discovering the connection between the cancer that killed her and the factory that employed her, I began to grieve again.

Soon after I made the connection, I drove out to the country to visit the cemetery where Mom's body had been laid to rest years earlier on a summer afternoon in 1974. Mom was not there because she was with Jesus. I parked next to a row of headstones and started walking until I found her grave, marked with a simple, small stone. The graves all around her's were decorated with flowers and mementos. Mom's grave was

Thelma three days before she passed

bare. It hit me all at once – a sad recognition of all the life events, the milestones, and the holidays we didn't share. I decided then and there that I would visit regularly and make sure her grave was decorated for every holiday.

I also decided I would make sure people knew what the factory had done to Mom.

Dad

Dad was born October 10, 1934 in Luttrell, Tennessee to Earl and Fern Dukes. Earl and Fern raised their large family deep in the hills of Tennessee. Fern fed her family from the land and often took

Glenn "Jerry" Dukes
in 1972, his hire-in year

in laundry to help clothe the kids while Earl worked. They packed their family up and moved to Indiana in 1950 in hopes of easier times and the promise of factory and construction jobs.

It's said that the difference between a career and a job is passion. Dad certainly made a career out of his devotion to Delco and General Motors. He worked in the paint department, served as a group

17

leader, and traveled to Mexico to train employees there in the plant Delco established to outsource work and reduce production costs. He drove only GM cars.

Though Dad found work very satisfying, he looked forward to retirement, and having dedicated his life to the plant, he could reasonably expect to retire comfortably, certainly not extravagantly, and spend his senior years enjoying NASCAR and his grandchildren. When he hung up his hat in the fall of 1999, he looked forward to a long retirement.

Nine years later, when Dad noticed he was bruising and tiring too easily and frequently felt breathless, he was referred to an oncologist who diagnosed him with Myelodysplastic Syndrome, or MDS, a rare condition that typically progresses into Acute Myeloid Leukemia. He was given a year to live.

That was the first time I had ever heard of Myelodysplastic Syndrome, and the first time I had heard the word benzene.

"Have you ever heard of benzene?" the oncologist asked my dad.

"Heard of it?" Dad said. "I used it every day at work for 30 years."

CHAPTER 2

WORKING WITH DEADLY CHEMICALS

What Is Benzene?

Benzene is recognized around the world as a Category A carcinogen. It is produced in large quantities in the United States for use in industry. In automotive factories like Delco, benzene is found in paints, solvents, adhesives and paint removers.

When inhaled, ingested or absorbed through the skin, benzene can cause cell mutation, which can lead to cancer. Benzene used in factories can pollute the air, pipelines, waterways, ground water, and soil, thereby endangering the general public just the same and sometimes more so than those who work in the factory.

Experts have recognized an association between benzene and a variety of blood diseases for more than 50 years, an assertion long corroborated by epidemiologic studies, animal data, and carcinogenic bioassays. Exposure to benzene can result in cancer or blood disease, such as leukemia, up to 40 years after contact. (Nachman Brautbar, 2006.) Long into retirement, former Delco employees are succumbing to diseases directly associated with benzene exposure, including various cancers, aplastic anemia, myelofibrosis, pancytopenia, and myelodysplasia syndrome; a precursor to acute myeloid leukemia.

What Is Trichloroethylene?

Trichloroethylene is a synthetic, light sensitive, volatile, colorless liquid that is miscible with many non-polar organic solvents. Trichloroethylene is used mainly as a degreaser for metal parts. Upon combustion, it produces irritants and toxic gases. Occupational exposure to trichloroethylene is associated with excess incidences of liver cancer, kidney cancer and non-Hodgkin lymphoma. It is reasonably anticipated to be a human carcinogen.

Plant 9 in Kokomo, Indiana. This is the plant Jerry worked in and is now referred to as "the graveyard."

Trichloroethylene is not thought to occur naturally in the environment. However, it has been found in underground water sources and many surface waters as a result of the manufacture, use, and disposal of the chemical. A lot of local retirees from Delco refer to the chemical as "trich" (pronounced "trike").

I've talked to a lot of workers who washed parts with this. It often ate right through their gloves. Unfortunately, some of them went onto develop rare bone cancers on their fingers and wrists. A lot of them suffered amputations of fingers due to the chemicals.

Dad's Exposure

Dad started working in Plant 7 in 1972 and then was moved to Plant 9. He was always a painter. His job was to run the paint machine. He set up the paint machines and booths at the beginning of the shift and kept them running throughout the shift. This included keeping the machines loaded with paint, disassembling the machine/booths and cleaning them throughout the shift. His co-workers called him the "chemical man."

The co-workers all clearly stated that NEVER, at anytime, were they offered protective masks until the mid 1980's. The co-workers further stated that while they were given rubber gloves to protect their hands from the paint, varnish and paint remover chemicals, the gloves provided little protection at the end of day because the fingers of the gloves would be eaten away from the chemicals. Dad would also have to go to the "oil house" and get these chemicals as part of his job. Co-workers stated that dad would use straight benzene as part of the cleaning process. During the course of my research I obtained proof of this on GM/Delco letterhead.

Dad told Erik (our attorney) and I at the initial meeting that he would have to get in these paint booths and run the machines while breathing heavy chemicals. At one point, Delco sent dad to Matamoros, Mexico for two weeks to teach the workers at the plant there how to set up the paint machines and booths. This was in or around 1980 and he

Glenn "Jerry" Dukes pictured last row on right. Group picture of his department in 1972 when he hired in.

stated that he wasn't offered any type of mask there either. County records showed 24 deaths in our county from acute myeloid leukemia (AML) from 2006-2009. Eight of those were confirmed workers. These records were obtained in December of 2010 and there were 6 more deaths from AML that year.

CHAPTER 3

DARK DAYS

The Diagnosis

It was late April, almost dusk, and I was outside with my family relaxing around a fire when the phone rang. I was expecting a call from my dad's oncologist, so I stepped inside the house for privacy. The day before, dad and I met with the oncologist for the first time, and she sent him for lab work and a bone marrow biopsy. Dad told her, "just call my daughter and tell her what's wrong with me, and she can explain it to me in a way that I can understand." He signed paperwork to appoint me as his healthcare POA.

When they asked him if he wanted a DNR - a "do not resuscitate" - he grabbed my arm and said, "I want all efforts, Sherry."

I wasn't really alarmed, because we didn't know what was wrong, just something amiss with his bloodwork. Dad's oncologist was also a hematologist.

So, when the phone rang, I was not overly worried and certainly not expecting what I was about to hear. I sat down at the dining room table as I took the call, enjoying the breeze from the open window. My gaze fell upon the tall pines that lined my backyard as the doctor spoke. Dad had myelodysplastic syndrome or MDS for short. It's classified as smoldering leukemia, she said, and there was a 50/50 chance it would evolve into Acute Myeloid Leukemia. She was concerned with dad's cytogenics report, which was the bone marrow biopsy. He was missing chromosomes and his DNA was altered from benzene exposure.

What does it all mean, I asked. She said he might live for another month, maybe 14.

I stared at the trees until I regained my composure. "I can't tell my dad he's going to die."

She recommended a trial drug that might extend Dad's life closer to that 14 months. I agreed without hesitation and established that we would not tell my dad the prognosis. "We will tell him he has a blood disorder that could get worse, and there is a drug we can use to try to prevent that," I said. I knew my dad, and if he lost hope, he would sit in his chair and wait to die. If he didn't know, perhaps the power of positive thinking would work to our advantage. I wasn't giving up hope.

I hung up the phone, still in shock. While I didn't have to tell my dad, I did have to tell my brothers and sisters and make sure they agreed to my plan. They did. The next morning my dad came for coffee like he always did, and I told him that he had a blood disorder called MDS and they were going to treat it with a chemotherapy trial drug even though it wasn't cancer. That was true - it wasn't actually leukemia yet.

He took it all in stride and didn't question anything. He had the infusions once a month and then lab work. Each time, the lab work looked better. We did this for five months. He tolerated the treatments well, and it didn't slow him down. He kept up with his usual activities and even took a couple of vacations. After his last infusion in September, I took him to the oncologist once a month for lab work and a check-up. Each month his lab work came back normal. I found myself believing my own lie.

Making The Connection

Dad began the experimental chemotherapy to prolong his life. I sat in the waiting room while he was hooked up to the tubes that would deliver a combination of agents into his blood in hopes of slowing the progress of his condition. I steeled myself for what I'd see when the nurse called me back to sit with Dad for the duration of the treatment, but the shock I felt had nothing to do with PICC lines and chemicals. I found Dad among friends.

To his left and to his right were two men just about Dad's age, and he introduced them to me as co-workers. I'll call them Bob and Marty.

"You're not going to believe this," Dad said, nodding to the gentleman on his right. "Bob was my foreman and Marty worked my line, and guess what? They have the same thing I do!"

I stood in shock as I tried to make sense of what I was hearing. Already I'd learned that Acute Myeloid Leukemia and its precursor, MDS, were caused by only three things: a history of chemotherapy, radiation, and benzene. My dad and his co-workers had only one thing in common, benzene.

I filed my suspicions away in the back of my mind and focused on what was important in the coming weeks. But it was there always, poking around in the part of my brain that sensed there was something not right about Dad's situation. Something more than the natural course of life and the certainty of death. Something unjust.

AML

I didn't have to wait long to know my feelings of injustice were founded. I had been asking a few questions around town and a family member of another worker reached out to me. This current autoworker for Delco Electronics in Kokomo knew that something wasn't right. He had unexplained bruising, weakness, and shortness of breath. He suspected that the toxic chemicals he had been exposed to on a daily basis were making him sick. He went to the plant medical facility and expressed his concern. The plant nurse drew some blood for lab work and told him he'd be notified of the results. A couple weeks later, he went back to the plant facility and asked for a copy of his labs. The plant nurse and doctor told him his labs were normal but they had misplaced them and couldn't give him a copy. He persisted for a couple weeks to no avail, then decided to go to his own physician, as his health was continuing to decline. Lab work was completed again by his own physician. The results were acute myeloid leukemia. He knew that other co-workers were sick like him. There were workers that had nervous system disorders, kidney failure and high and low white blood cell counts. He knew the plant medical facility was trying to hide his lab results. When he finally did receive them, the results were the same as his own physician's. He wrote legislators and OSHA to no avail. He was harassed at work by his peers for trying to bring attention to this problem. One day his foreman pulled him aside and said, "Why don't you just retire." Unfortunately, he did retire to an early death from toxic exposure.

Acute myeloid leukemia is a rare cancer of the blood. An etiologic association between benzene and diseases of the blood was shown more than 50 years ago, and has since been corroborated by epidemiologic studies, animal data, and by carcinogenic bioassays. Benzene is now considered, by national and international scientific and health organizations, to be a human carcinogen. It can take up to 40 years after first being exposed to manifest itself as leukemia or another long list of blood disorders caused by benzene exposure. (Nachman Brautbar, 2006.) Hence, this is why retirees of Delco/GM are now becoming sick and dying of cancers, leukemias and other blood disorders caused by benzene and other toxic chemicals. Other diseases caused by benzene exposure are aplastic anemia, myelofibrosis, pancytopenia, and the myelodyplastic syndrome, as noted earlier. Myelodyplastic syndrome is actually a precursor to acute myeloid leukemia.

Benzene is produced in large quantities in the United States. In the auto industry it is found in paints, solvents, adhesives and paint removers. In 1978 OSHA stepped in to reduce the permissible workplace exposure to benzene but what about the workers who were exposed in the 1950's, 1960's and 1970's? These factories exposed them and knew it was unsafe. Who is accountable and what lies in the soil underneath and around these factories? Is it another Love Canal disaster waiting to be exposed?

A female retiree who wishes to remain anonymous, said miscarriages, hysterectomies, and breast cancer ran rampant among the female employees. Men were being diagnosed with testicular and bladder cancers. Men and woman both were being targeted by colon, pancreatic, stomach and esophagus cancers, as well as respiratory problems. When exposed to low to moderate amounts of benzene on a daily basis, it can take 20 to 40 years after the first exposure for these diseases and cancers to manifest themselves. Benzene was just one of many chemicals in the toxic soup to which these workers were exposed.

CHAPTER 4

FACING THE INEVITABLE

Personal Injury

Dad didn't want to sue anyone. He always taught us to avoid confrontation and that it was best to turn the other cheek. He was also fiercely loyal to his employer, Delco Electronics. Once he had fully gained his strength back, we convinced him to talk to a lawyer. Dad was skeptical, but we were angry. I couldn't get past the fact that dad went into that factory every day to support us, and this was the end of it.

His livelihood would cost him his life. His kids had no problem wanting someone to pay for that.

In March of 2009, I contacted a local lawyer whose response was, "I believe you've got a good case, but I have to live and do business in this town." He did, however, refer us to a firm in Indianapolis with lawyers who wanted to meet with dad. This firm brought in a young, but experienced, benzene lawyer from Texas named Eric. We set up a meeting at my house. Dad didn't really trust or like lawyers, and he told this young Texan as much.

"Well, Mr. Dukes, what do you like?" Erick asked.

Dad said, " I like to watch Andy Griffith everyday at noon."

Erick stood and, just like the TV show, he whistled the theme song to Andy Griffith.

Dad said, "Hey I like you. Give me the papers and I will sign."

Before the meeting ended, Erick advised Dad to put in place a Power of Attorney (POA) to act on his behalf if he became

incapacitated and write a codicil to his current will naming benefi-
ciaries should something happen to him, to designate any proceeds
that might come from the pending personal injury lawsuit. This was
an important piece of advice that dad followed. Although he had
remarried twice since losing his young Thelma so many years ago, he
wanted to make sure his children were protected.

Wrongful Death

My siblings all lived out of state except one brother. Every May
they all made the trip back to Indiana for the Indianapolis 500 and
a family reunion. Dad was always so excited to have all his kids back
home under one roof even for just a long weekend.

April was uneventful, lab work normal. The routine was always
the same. I would take dad in for his lab work and the next day we
would see the doctor for a check-up. Now, dad could drive himself
but he just wanted me to take him. I was in nursing school and
I think it gave dad some kind of security for me to tag along. I
wouldn't have had it any other way. Losing my mom at such a young
age had made me a daddy's girl and protective over him.

I had taken him in for labs on May 11th. My routine was to
always go back by and get a copy of the lab report before the next
day's appointment. Being a nursing student I knew how to read a lab
report. I also knew everything there was to know about MDS and
Acute Myeloid Leukemia as I had thoroughly researched it. Today
was no different. I walked in, got the report, and was looking at it as I
walking out.

The first thing I saw was a high white cell count and as my eyes
followed down, I saw blasts. I stopped and sat down in the first chair
because the room was spinning. My hands were trembling and I was
trying to focus on this really cool fish aquarium in the waiting room
until I regained my composure. Once I did, I looked at the report
again. I knew what a high white count and blasts meant. Dad had
developed Acute Myeloid Leukemia.

I walked up to the receptionist and asked her to have the oncologist call me today because I wanted to talk to her before dad's

appointment tomorrow. My phone rang that evening at 7:06. I call these moments "defining memories" because whether it's something profoundly good or bad, we seem to remember every detail of these events. I spoke first and I said, "I saw blasts present in his report today. Does that mean what I think it does?" She said, "Sherry, I'm sorry, he's developed Acute Myeloid Leukemia." She went onto say that he would decline quickly and he had about 6-8 weeks to live. Blood transfusions would help keep him comfortable for a short time but we couldn't do them indefinitely. She said, we have to tell him tomorrow that his blood disorder has gotten worse.

I hung up the phone and just sat there for a minute. I had five young children in their rooms and my husband was still at work. As a mother, even in catastrophic situations, you just don't breakdown in front of your kids. I would have my breakdown after I got them to bed.

As I got up from the chair, I could feel the weight of the lie we carried over the last year. A couple hours later after the kids were all in bed, I sat down and cried. I selfishly cried for myself and then I cried for my dad and all those who loved him. Then I cried for the unfairness of it all. I thought about the decision to not tell him the real prognosis 12 months earlier. I didn't regret it. I didn't feel guilty. My siblings and I were the only ones who knew. We carried that truth with us for a year. While it was a heavy load to carry, it wasn't a burden. It was a gift from us to him. He had had the best year, but tomorrow we had to tell him that he had only 6-8 weeks to live. That's no time for anyone to prepare. It's not time for those of us who love him to prepare.

I was saved in that Baptist church as a young girl but I know I can't be the only one who asks this question... I just want to know if people have to die, why does it have to be good people, why not the mean people? I've asked a lot of people that question and more often than not the answer is "God takes the good ones home so they don't have to live in this bad world." I don't buy that answer. The world needs these good people. We need dad.

I called my brothers and sisters after I had regained my compo-sure to let them know. I took dad for his check-up the next day. The oncologist explained to him that the MDS had turned into Acute Myeloid Leukemia and that he had 6-8 weeks to live. Dad wasn't a candidate for a bone marrow transplant or any other treatments because of his age and he wouldn't survive the treatment.

I watched tears well up in his brown eyes and it was more than I could take. He said, "There has to be something I can try." She said that there were other clinical trials and she could refer him down to Indianapolis to The Simon Cancer Institute to see if he would qualify. Dad quickly agreed. I could see the desperation in his face. She walked out to get the referral and he said, "Sherry if I could just get a couple more years. I don't want anyone giving up on me. All efforts, Sherry, all efforts." I said, "Dad, I got you."

The first crisis we had to address is that dad's platelet count was less than 5,000. A normal platelet count is between 140,000-400,000. Platelets are important because they clump together and keep you from bleeding out when you have an injury. Dad was at high risk for internal bleeding from the slightest injury. Red blood cells circulate oxygen and when you don't have enough of those then you become short of breath. I was shocked when she asked dad to open his mouth and it was full of big black blood blisters. This was caused from the lack of platelets. So first order at hand was to get him some blood transfusions.

Shane and Dad on Shane's wedding day, three weeks before Dad's passing

She warned us that the transfusions were a temporary fix and although he'd feel good for a couple days, he would then decline and eventually the transfusions would stop helping. What happens in Acute leukemia is the blasts are immature white blood cells that never mature. They keep multiplying and crowd out the good blood cells.

The following week we went down to Simon Cancer Institute in Indianapolis. It didn't go well. The doctor there didn't have the best bedside manner and he very straightforward told dad he was dying and didn't qualify for any trials. We walked out of there and dad said,

"Don't ever take me to see Dr. Death again."

My brothers and sister arrived for Memorial Day Weekend and the Indianapolis 500. We had all talked beforehand and agreed we were going to put up a positive front for dad. Our youngest brother, Shane, had gotten engaged and had planned an October wedding. Knowing dad wouldn't be with us then, plans started rolling for a June wedding.

Shane and dad had a unique and close bond. It was important to both of them for dad to be his best man. The wedding was planned for 3 weeks later on June 20th. I could see dad was getting weaker everyday but he never complained. I didn't want to think about what was to come. I spent everyday with him and we never talked about death. I knew he wasn't ready, he had made that clear. At this point I wanted him to make it to Shane's wedding for both of them.

The wedding weekend came. Dad's oncologist set up for him to have a blood transfusion at 5 am the morning of the wedding. Dad woke up early and excited for the day. As he hopped in the car to go to the hospital, he said, "Let's go get me gassed up." That's how he referred to his blood transfusions. It was a wonderful day of family and celebrating. Dad looked normal on the outside. The next day was Father's Day and we continued to celebrate with a family cook out. Everyone traveled back home, all of us hugging and lingering just a little longer.

The next couple of weeks were uneventful but the morning of Monday July 6th, unknowing at the time, would mark the beginning of the end. Dad, like most men, was stubborn and independent. He decided to take a shower when he was home alone. He got weak and dizzy and fell in the shower. The next day he collapsed and was taken to the hospital. Tests revealed that he had a hematoma and was bleeding internally due to the fall. I can still hear his horrible moaning at the hospital. I had never seen my dad in that kind of pain.

He was admitted to the hospital and the oncologist came in to see him. She stood at his bedside and put her hand on his and explained to him that he was bleeding internally from the fall and to give him more transfusions would be futile. She suggested we take him home on hospice.

Dad immediately spoke up and said, "No one is giving up on me, are you telling me I'm dying?" I will never forget her gentle, soft-spoken response. She said, "Mr. Dukes, I'm just a doctor. I'm not Jesus. I don't have the final say and we know with Jesus anything is possible." That was so profound to me because all any of us have in this world is hope in any situation. If we don't have hope, we might as well give up. I was so grateful to her for choosing her words as to not take away any hope he was clinging to. Dad's response after that was, "Alright, let's go home."

I went home to get some sleep. I no sooner got home when dad called from the hospital. He said, "I'm worried, will you come back and sit with me?" I said, "Dad, you have no worries because I've got all your worries and yes, I'm on my way." This is important because any time anyone called dad with a need, his response was "I'm on my way," and he'd hang up the phone. I have always been a worrier and dad would say, "Sherry, you have no worries because I worry for you." I was so honored to be able to just once pay that back to him.

I called my siblings and told them to come back home. We got dad home and comfortable with hospice. If there was any blessing in this it was that dad was alert and able to visit with all of us. Anyone who knew dad knew that everyday he could be found sitting on his front porch, waving at every single car as if he'd known them his whole life. The day before he passed was no different. He was medicated with morphine but still able to walk out to the porch himself. He ate with us, drank his coffee, and smoked his cigarettes. Family stopped by to see him all day and into the evening, some of them traveling from his home state of Tennessee.

At one point dad leaned over to me and said, "I can't believe all these people are coming to see me." I said, "Dad, they love you. You have impacted a lot of people with your love throughout your lifetime." After everyone left except us kids, it was about 10 pm. I think he knew his time was close because he wanted to stay on the porch, so that's what we did. We had a great time talking and just sitting until 3 in the morning.

Ever since we were young, dad would break out into what he called "the jig." I always thought it was the hillbilly version of the twist. It always made us laugh. As we all followed dad into the house, much to our amazement, dad broke out in the jig and turned back to smile at us. It was a blessing and we loved that he did that for us kids one last time.

His hospital bed was in the living room so we got him settled into bed about 4:00 am and we all piled on the couches and chairs to sleep. About 2 hours later I noticed dad moaning and his breathing had changed. He was restless. I went over to his bedside to comfort him.

The next moments will haunt me everyday of my life. He looked at me wide-eyed and grabbed my hand. He said, "You need to do something because I'm not ready." Those were the last words he said to me. He drifted into unconsciousness and passed away a couple hours later. Everyday I see that image and hear those words. Personal Injury had just become Wrongful Death.

CHAPTER 5

FINDING PURPOSE

After Dad

Leukemia took Dad from us on a hot Saturday morning in July, 35 years to the day after the death of his pretty, young Thelma.

The day we buried Dad was the day I started my career as an environmental activist.

In the days and weeks following the funeral, I grieved as one would expect. I knew there was a connection between Dad's work at Delco and his death. Whereas my teen years were marked with a deep sadness because I couldn't remember my mom, in the weeks following Dad's death I was tormented by memories that caused my heart to ache. I couldn't not remember.

The day I discovered those papers about Mom's death and recognized the role the plant played in her cancer, grief begin to give way to anger. I lost both of my parents prematurely to a cancer caused by chemical exposure at the plant. I gave it a name: Delco Death.

Grief serves a healthy purpose, I believe, and given time, it eases just a bit and gives way to bittersweet memories. Anger is dangerous. If allowed to take root, it grows and consumes and invades all the sweet places in your heart once reserved for the memories that help you heal. There came a day when I realized I had to funnel my anger into something that would serve a purpose, something that would turn my pain into something positive. I was working toward a nursing degree; I decided to minor in environmental science.

The day I made that decision, I felt something like relief for the first time in months. I sat down that evening to watch television and enjoy this respite. Thumbing through the TV guide, I found a movie titled *Erin Brockovich* and watched it for the first time. Then I watched it again.

Erin Brockovich

My unexpected journey into activism started with a trip to the store to purchase notebooks, pens, and a satchel. I started my research knowing so very little about research methodologies. I was naïve and optimistic.

I went to the local newspaper and told a reporter about my dad and his co-workers, and I suspected he'd find many others like them if he'd take this story on. He said to me, "We all know there are a lot of sick factory workers out there, but we have an unwritten rule around here; we don't write about it."

Why?

"We don't want to draw attention to them, because we think more will come forward."

It didn't take long to lose my naivety, but I remained optimistic, and I finally found a reporter at another newspaper who was willing to entertain the possibility that I was onto something. We poured through records at the health department and found more deaths resulting from rare forms of leukemia, and not all of the victims were factory employees. He ran with it, publishing what would be the first article of its kind in Kokomo, a piece that barely scratched the surface but served to stir up enough interest to generate a database of anecdotal evidence to support my theory that Delco, and perhaps other factories, were responsible for many deaths. That reporter would tell me years later that the paper he wrote for was nervous about publishing the story.

I received one phone call after another from factory employees and former employees who were sick or had suffered from one form of cancer or another. One caller led me to a small group of retired Delco employees – guards, foremen and line workers – who wanted to share with me the results of their own investigation.

I remember thinking this was the break I'd been looking for.

I thought this was everything I needed to expose Delco for putting so many lives at risk.

Then the caller said something that sent chills up my spine.

"We'll meet you at 1:00 AM at the Waffle House. We'll be in the back booth. Come alone."

Not without trepidation, I met them the next morning. I slid into the last booth, pulled a notebook out of my satchel and began taking notes.

Over the next few months, I'd fill one notebook after another with first-hand accounts from victims, witnesses, and family members. Page after page of eye-witness accounts of corruption and malfeasance in one plant or another. Most of the names you will read have been changed to protect the identities of people who've no desire to step outside their anonymity or capitalize on their experience. Their stories are true and, as you'll see, they've been thoroughly vetted and substantiated using internal company memos, personnel notes, documents, and guard shack logs.

I'm here to tell their stories in hopes of giving a voice to their hurt and anger and disappointment. In doing so, I hope I honor the memories of Jerry and Thelma, who aspired to nothing more than a humble and comfortable life surrounded by family and friends.

The Meeting, 2011

Like something out of a movie, I met for the first time with that group of grass roots amateur senior detectives at 1:00 AM in the back booth at Waffle House. An older woman emerged as the spokesperson early on, but the others chimed in frequently. They worked at the plant in the 60s, 70s and 80s, and they relayed the things they saw that they knew were wrong. They promised me evidence to support their accusations.

The spokeswoman, we'll call her Jean, interrupted the conversation to warn me that digging around for information was dangerous. I needed to be careful, she said, to keep a low profile and be careful about who I talked to and who I shared my research with. She leaned toward me and asked, "Do you have a permit to carry, because you're going to need protection if you're really going to do this."

That gave me pause. Was I really going to do this? What was "this," exactly? I started this journey to find justice for Dad and Mom, to see if there were others who died as they did, because of exposure to dangerous chemicals. Was I really in danger?

They seemed to think so. Jean's home had been ransacked several times, and most of those present that night at Waffle House had received threatening phone calls designed to stop them from pursuing their detective work. For the most part, they did just that, only coming out of retirement to share their experiences with me.

One gentleman laid a binder on the table as he told me he had been employed as a guard at one of the back gates.

"They were dumping," he said.

"They were dumping?" I asked.

Truck drivers would use the back gate to haul loads of chemicals – benzene and trich – to a waste collection site, where the plant paid to dispose of these deadly chemicals. It was understood that if the driver could find a place to dump his load undetected, someplace other than the collection site, he would get a bonus. Bribing drivers was cheaper than paying for what passed at that time as proper disposal.

"Some of it was dumped behind the plant," he said. "We call it the big green monster underneath the plant."

Another gentleman, also a guard, said he worked at the Plant 8 boiler room Friday afternoons while "upper management" played poker and discussed local dump locations.

One of the women said, "For all us women, it wasn't a matter of if you got cancer, but when. We had miscarriages, breast cancer, uterine cancer, ovarian cancer, fertility problems… We'd go to the plant doctor, and he would say we brought it on ourselves because we smoked." Another female said that women of childbearing years were discouraged from working in certain departments.

When the women started suffering from nose bleeds and headaches, the union leader brought in a device to check the air quality. He reported to the plant manager that the sensor indicated dangerous levels of arsenic and trich. The plant manager dismissed the complaint, insisting the air was fine, and told the employees to get back to work. When one of the ladies was transported to the hospital by ambulance after collapsing at the plant, the manager threatened to fire anyone who mentioned the air quality complaints. He told the paramedics the victim had a "pre-existing health condition."

Another woman they told me about was Jenny, who worked in what was called "the clean room." Jenny recalled walking to her car one day after work. She hadn't been feeling quite right for months but couldn't put her finger on any one symptom. She was 34 years old at the time. As Jenny walked to her car that day, she said she started to feel weird and her vision tunneled in. She made it to her car and made an appointment with her doctor the next day. After a battery of tests, she was diagnosed with advanced ovarian cancer. Jenny said the chemicals would make her eyes burn.

The ceilings, although they appeared to have ventilation, consisted of pipes running into false ceilings to give the appearance that the chemicals were being directed outside. But, the fumes were "hovering in space," if you will, above the workers. Jenny also said, "Sometimes when 2 or 3 people would get the same cancer in a department, we knew it. The maintenance people would come in and disassemble all the machinery and tear up the floors. Those departments would get shut down."

CHAPTER 6

DISCOVERY AND SETTLEMENT

The Case and Still Covering Up

Soon after that clandestine meeting, I went to the plant to get Dad's employment records. I had to know the departments he'd worked in, the names of the chemicals to which he'd been exposed, and the companies that produced them. This was the first part of discovery. You see, in Indiana, you can't sue your employer for toxic exposure unless you can prove malicious intent. That's why factories like to set up shop in Indiana. You can sue the chemical companies that provided the chemicals. Identifying the chemicals dad was exposed to and the co-workers who could place him with the chemicals were key to the wrongful death case. I had collected enough information to know there was malicious intent, but I understood the law. Still in the back of my mind, I couldn't shake the stories I had been told.

I knew this information should be available, having it on good authority from a former plant Healthy and Safety Manager that those records were still stored on site. Unfortunately, the current Health and Safety Manager denied it and insisted he didn't have access to my dad's records.

It took only one call to Detroit to get my dad's records emailed to me in their entirety. The really nice lady who answered the phone seemed happy to help, and I've often hoped she was never reprimanded, or worse, for helping me.

Soon after, I was put in touch with a friend of a friend who was still working in the plant's Health and Safety office. He confirmed for me that the chemical records from the 60s, 70s and 80s were still filed on site. Over the course of several days, my new friend made copies of these records and delivered them to me after work. The records amounted to hundreds of pages, so we spread the operation out over several days so as not to raise suspicion in the office. These people were all too willing to help because, like my family, they had lost loved ones from the affects of these chemicals.

Not long after, I got a call from the plant manager who said, "I understand you requested your dad's employment records. I'm sorry we have no records from 1999. We don't have record of him working here as far as that goes. We don't keep records in Health and Safety from that time period."

I thanked him for calling and assured him I'd received all my dad's employment records and the Health and Safety records I'd requested. His tone changed dramatically.

"I've heard about you," he said, "and I'd like to know just what your agenda is."

"Just the truth," I said.

And now I knew for sure they were trying to keep it covered. On December 7, 2009, a wrongful death case was filed in New Jersey on behalf of my dad. It was a cold, snowy morning in Indiana. I remember sitting at my desk at home, looking out the same window at the big snow flakes falling against the pines trees. The same trees I was looking at when I got the call about dad's diagnosis. It was a win day for dad.

Finding Co-Workers

The next phase of discovery would be locating co-workers to associate dad with these products. I thought this would be the easy part. Although dad had retired years before, he kept in contact and met monthly for dinner with a group of people he had worked with. I started with those people. Some of them I had known since I was a young girl. These were people who had worked closely with dad on a daily basis. These people had become good friends over the years.

I was met with resistance. Some of them were older and just couldn't remember important facts. Some of them feared retaliation for talking. Some of them had been misled and told "we were just greedy kids." Unfortunately, these were the co-workers that could have helped the most.

I knew my heart was in the right place on this journey. My siblings and I wanted these companies to pay for dad's death. I learned early on in his case that these companies would never publicly admit wrong doing or apologize. Their only form of apology would come in a monetary settlement. Little did I know it would take almost 7 more years of investigating to track down co-workers willing to go on record.

Fortunately, dad had been well known and liked in the plant. It started with phone calls to one or two people who would say, "Hey, I remember your dad and this or that person will be able to help you." It was a journey of sorts. I still met resistance along the way. Sometimes I resorted to door-knocking with dad's picture in tow and telling his story.

In January of 2017, depositions were taken and the companies settled. I thought I would feel relief and closure but I didn't. I realized that I was at the beginning of a new journey. All the people that I had met and talked to along the way were counting on me to be their voice. I wasn't going to let them down. Their stories and losses were no less important than mine. I thought about dad and what he would do. Dad was a giver and a helper. He would say to use what I have collected to help others. I looked at the stack of totes sitting beside my desk; totes full of documents, research, and stories from workers of bad conditions. I realized

A segment of the complaint filed due to the wrongful death of Glenn Dukes

I had to keep going. I could use my years of discovery to help other sick co-workers and their families get justice. This would create a legacy that would honor both of my parents.

Employees Tell Their Stories

Through my research, a long-time employee stated that records as far back as the early 1970s were kept on site until being moved to Indianapolis, Indiana to a storage facility called Now Records.

The employee believed these records all still existed at this location. We would later confirm this and the judge ordered GM to produce these records, but not until after GM would deny the records existed, and eventually got reprimanded by the court.

Joe, a co-worker, told me that his job inside the plant was to dispose of unused and recycled chemicals which included benzene and trich among others. He stated that he was instructed to do this by pouring the chemicals down pipes hidden in the wall corridors of the plant. He now suffers from a neurological/nerve disorder that his physicians have said was related to exposure from these chemicals.

An, upper management retiree from GM/Delco stated that there are two locations of buried toxic barrels on the 31 plant site. One location is at Plant 9 (before Plant 9 was built) while Plants 7, 8 and 10 were in operation. The other site of buried waste is at the backside of the plant where offices are located. I believe this information to be true as over the years some of those who are sick with rare cancers and have reached out to me

Townhall Meeting I organized in January of 2019 for retirees to voice their concerns

were office workers on the backside of the plant who never stepped foot in the plant.

Previous members of upper management also confirmed what other retirees have told me in regards to chemicals being dumped inside the plant grounds. I also would like to note that a groundwater supply adjacent to the factory towards the south has been flagged for unsafe levels of Benzene several times according to Water Safety Data Reports during that time. There are periodic drilling sites set up around the perimeter of the plant. According to upper management employees at the time who wish to remain anonymous, a clean, safe reading could not be obtained anywhere. This would corroborate reports of chemicals being buried on the site. The reason for this drilling could have something to do with the recent sales of the property by Delphi Delco to GM.

Retirees have stated to me that they were instructed to cover up hazardous waste stickers on chemical barrels with brown paper. The flooring was torn up periodically and replaced in Plant 9 whenever two or more people became sick with the same cancer or disease. On one occasion when this happened, several employees had begun losing their eyelashes, eyebrows and pubic hair. Also, whenever two or more employees on a line became ill with cancer, that line was shutdown and a local steel company was called in to remove the machinery.

Retired guards from the plant reported that truck drivers were given bonuses if they could dispose of the chemicals going out of the plant before getting to the hazmat location. They said the truck drivers often boasted about "it being a good night." These incidences always took place at night and, if possible, without being detected, the chemicals were dumped in our creek. It has always been a well known fact that our creeks here are contaminated and there are even signs posted. This was always blamed on the Continental Steel Company, but I am now sure that Delco played a part in this, too.

A janitor stated that the ceilings inside the plant where the ventilation pipes went were actually there to provide a false sense of security for the workers because the ceilings were drop ceilings and there was approximately 20 feet of free space stuffed with insulation to catch the chemicals.

One retiree said she was working alongside an employee who kept going to his supervisor and telling him that the ventilation wasn't working and that the fumes were going in his face. One day at the plant, this man collapsed and died from it. When the paramedics arrived, the plant nurse lied and told them the man had an asthma attack (this man did not suffer from asthma). The employees who witnessed it were instructed to keep quiet.

CHAPTER 7

CASTING A WIDER NET

Old Timers

In spite of my fear, I thoroughly enjoyed meeting the people who wanted to share their experiences with me. Their stories were different, but mostly they all ended the same way, with the loss of someone they loved. It was a rare interview that ended on a good note.

The reporter I worked with warned me that people would love me or hate me for the ongoing work and research I was doing. I've been fortunate, I think.

Oddly enough, because I am a history buff, I've found myself enjoying the stories from the "old timers" who recall the early days, when Delco was in its heyday. I find my mind connects the growth and development of the plant with the history of the town I love. It's only when the stories turn personal that I can separate the history from the mystery of corporate greed and malfeasance.

Jim worked in Plant 10 in 1964, where from his third-floor window on the north side of the building, he could watch the construction of the new plant on U.S. 31. "I had an excellent view," he said. "I watched many barrels being carted out of Plant 8 over to where the new plant was being built. They were dropped there and buried, and they built on top of them. I can't even begin to guess how many hundreds of barrels were buried that summer."

Plant 9 sits empty today and is accurately referred to as the "graveyard" by retirees.

Robert told me there were pipes hidden in the walls and corridors. "Chemicals were dumped down those pipes," he said.

"We knew it was wrong. We didn't know where the pipes went. We just did what we were told to do." Pipes ran up and into the drop ceilings, giving the illusion of ventilation, but Robert noted that fumes rose from the pipes and seemed to hover at the ceiling above his head.

Manny was a former guard who said there was a very big red pipe in the basement that ran to the west behind a locked fence where a guard stood watch. "There was talk," Manny said. "We all thought wasted chemicals were being piped out underground."

A retired janitor told me, "When multiple people got the same sickness or cancer, they would shut down the whole department, rip up the floors, and remove the equipment."

Another retiree recalled one night when the floors were being worked on and the entire third shift was suddenly evacuated to the Plant 8 medical center. Some were transported to local hospitals. No one ever explained it to the employees.

A maintenance worker told me there were always dead birds on the roof of the plant.

I've talked to several former employees who suffered from bone cancer. They told me trich would eat through their gloves.

From another worker from plant 9, "I saw the air be so hazy in plant 9. They would open the windows way up close to the ceiling. People called the union. We called it 'the zone.' We called health and safety. And we were told some one would come from the environmental agency to test the air. We had faith they would help us all. The trouble was they gave GM notice when they were coming in. They would come around and open all the windows to let the fog out. We didn't get any help. Ever. So many people have died from cancer. Blood disorders. I had breast cancer. And people, I think, still die over this. But we were never warned about the chemicals. Now my daughter has cancer. She worked for GM for 20 years. Did it come from there? Not sure. We will never know."

Everyone I ever spoke with either commented along the way or ended the conversation with "No one ever warned us that these chemicals were bad for us."

The Farmer

One day I got a call from a sweet woman who started to cry as she told me about her battle with chronic leukemia. Like so many of these dear people who share their stories, she reminded me of my dad. They all seem to share the same incredible work ethic and a fierce loyalty to the plant that gave them a paycheck. In so many ways, these callers grieved for the loss of their innocence. They believed their hard work would be rewarded, and they believed their employers were good people.

This woman was heartbroken, and she begged me, "Please listen and go check this out. There is farmland south of Kokomo, and Delco signed a lease with the farmer back in the 70s to use some of his land. The farmer died, but his widow is still there."

I thanked her and hung up the phone. It sounded a bit far-fetched to me and I had become accustomed to shocking stories. A couple of weeks past, and when I couldn't shake the memory of her call, I decided to take a drive to the country. I spied a farmer working in his barn, an older gentleman, and I guessed he'd lived there long enough to know his neighbors.

I wasn't sure how to approach him. Even as I approached him, I didn't know how to approach him. I have no idea where it came from, but I blurted out that I was a journalist writing a story about the leukemia deaths at the old Delco Plant. I told him I got a tip that Delco leased some nearby land years ago and was dumping on the land. The man yelled to his wife, "Bring us something cold to drink." Then he looked at me and said, "You better sit down over there on the tractor."

"You've been told right," he said. "The farmer leased the land to Delco. After a while, birds started dying, and chickens, and other livestock. Then the farmer died. His widow is still alive. None of us around here know what to do. The paper wrote a small paragraph about the mysterious deaths of animals and birds on the back page about 25 years ago, and nothing was ever said or done."

I asked him if he could show me where it was, and he led me down the road a piece, where he pointed down a long lane and said,

"What you're looking for is at the end of this lane, but remember, you're on private property."

After he drove away, I paused just a minute to ponder the implications of what I was about to do. Then I did it.

I sped down the gravel lane until I reached a clearing, where I found a tall barbed wire fence and woods beyond. Tucked inside the fence was a dock, surrounded by what looked to be oily, slick soil.

I got the hell out of there.

The Phone Call

One night, I got a call from a friend, who said simply, "You're going to want to come over."

There I met an older couple, the husband riddled with cancer, and the wife ready and anxious to tell me about his illness and his time at Delco.

"We have something for you," she said.

The lady kept a letter in the safe at home. The envelope, addressed to her husband, had no return address. Inside was a single sheet of Delco letterhead, an interoffice memo between two people stating there had been exposure at the plant, and it listed the names of the employees exposed. It read: This is for interoffice only. We cannot rule out human casualties from this exposure.

Every employee on the list was dead, except two. This man was on the list, and he was dying.

"The Big Green Monster"

Eight years passed. Eight years I chased clues and stories. I carry the same satchel, and I've filled one notebook after another, filing them away one by one in a rubber tote. I know their contents by heart. I know the stories that fill the pages. I've cried over them. I cried with the people who shared their stories and cried as I wrote them down. I told them all about my dad.

I thought I could no longer be shocked. I thought I'd heard it all. Until the day I got a phone call from a gentleman who had worked at Delco as a Security Supervisor. He was battling cancer.

He made regular rounds in the 70s and 80s following a route that took him into "the warehouse – near the old building where they sell antiques now - across the bridge, then to the right up the hill and there is another set of buildings Delco occupied back then." Some of the buildings were used to store chemicals. These buildings are conveniently located by the Wildcat Creek. "One night, my co-worker and I were making the rounds in the warehouse, and we came across this huge hatch we hadn't seen before. There was usually stuff stored there, and I guess it covered the hatch. We lifted it, and there was a tunnel. Curiosity go the better of us, so we walked down into it and followed it till it came out at Wildcat Creek. I knew there were trucks coming in and out of the warehouse every day. I knew they were dumping in there. I reported it, and the next thing I knew, the hatch was sealed, and I was transferred out of state."

Early in his career, he'd worked at Plant 1, where he saw first hand they were dumping chemicals underground. "They put enough chemicals in there to make it look like it was safe to dump if it was checked. It went underground in the neighborhood by the government houses."

I knew there were people living in this area that have leukemia; several have reached out to me.

I hung up and drove over to the warehouse. The whole area is part of a cleanup project. A casual observer would assume the building is abandoned, but I drove around back and spotted semi-trucks with a name on the side. I called the company and inquired about a job as a driver. That's how I learned they were affiliated with GM. I asked what I'd be hauling. "Just auto stuff," he said, and he hung up when I pressed for more information.

Soon after, I got a call from a woman who worked in the Plant 1 area. "They put me in a room to clean, and there were big tanks. I heard what sounded like water running under the drains, so I lifted one of the drains, and there was a green liquid flowing fast under there. I reported it because there had been eight women from our department diagnosed with breast cancer. They told us it was safe and unrelated. Later, they started sending all the women to breast cancer awareness class.

GM is no stranger to being confronted about dumping toxic waste. The GM foundry division plant located in St. Lawrence County, New York, opened in 1958. In 1983, the EPA released a directive stating that this GM plant posed a major menace to human health. It was ultimately placed on the EPA's Superfund national priority list as a hazardous waste site. In 2009, Christopher Amato, deputy chief of the attorney general's bureau, charged that GM had "basically flouted the law for 25 years." This was in regard to GM's contamination of the St. Lawrence River, Raquette River, and nearby St. Regis Mohawk Indian Reservation. The issue concerned GM enough that they gave residents bottled water, even as they refused to admit to any wrongdoing.

In 1988, workers in GM's Lordstown, Ohio, factory, concerned about factory death rates, formed a group called Workers Against Toxic Waste and created the Lordstown Memorial, which lists the names of deceased employees of the plant in Lordstown.

They demanded a study be done, and though GM staunchly refused accountability, the study results revealed stomach and pancreatic cancer at 6.7 and 3.3 times the expected rate. A multinational report in 1990 stated that more than three million pounds of toxic chemicals were released from this factory. GM was fined 1.5 million dollars for this incident alone.

It is easy for factories like GM to deny wrongdoing. It's easy to pay a fine, deny the charges, and ignore the human cost.

In cities and towns where these factories operate, Americans depend on the jobs and the tax revenue to help finance local government and services.

Kokomo is no different. What is GM's response to the retirees who are becoming ill from toxic exposure? They shrug and shirk responsibility. A March, 2000 report released by Sanford University said GM's Delphi plant released 603,900 pounds of toxic chemicals into the environment in 1994.

What lies beneath the 3.9 million square foot plant in Kokomo? Local retirees say "the big green monster." In 1993, CEO Gary Diskinson referred to the company as a "500-pound gorilla." This 500-pound toxic gorilla is slowly awakening. A day of reckoning is coming when this giant gorilla fully awakens in this factory town.

This is a matter of life or death, for the workers who have died, and those who are facing illness now and the health risks to our community. This isn't about jobs and the economy. It's about the land, the water we drink, the air we breathe and the bodies we live in.

It is a tragedy and a human rights issue.

CHAPTER 8

LOOKING AHEAD

Beyond The Factory

Malicious intent refers to the intent, without just cause or reason, to commit a wrongful act that will result in harm to another. It is the intent to harm or do some evil purpose. After I finished the work for dad's case, I turned back to malicious intent. I knew from what the retirees told me that this was clearly the case. I was getting more phone calls from people who didn't work at the factory, but were sick with these same cancers. One example locally is Plant 5.

Plant 5 was located on the north end of town. I visited with some of the families that live in the neighborhood east of this site. These families have dealt with aggressive cancers, women with reproductive tumors, infertility, multiple miscarriages and the list goes on. These people were first notified about 6 years ago of possible contamination. Homes were tested by the EPA and found to have unsafe vapors of TCE and PCE gases. One individual I met with has suffered an array of medical problems. The EPA admitted that there were unsafe levels of both TCE and PCE in their home. The EPA agreed to put a mitigation system in to correct the problem. However, this person had to fight for two years for the air results and system to be installed. Documentation exists showing that numerous attempts at contacting the EPA through phone calls, emails, and snail mail went unanswered. All the while this family was living in an unsafe environment. Finally almost 4 years later, they showed up to install the system and conveniently put a "RACER Trust" sign up just before contacting them (see page 57).

You might think to yourself, "Why didn't they get out of the house?" It's documented that this contamination was known about 20 years ago, yet some of these people purchased their homes 10-15 years ago and this was not disclosed. These are working people with families. They have mortgages to pay. Where are they supposed to go and how much value do you think their home has now?

This is just one area here in Kokomo that is a problem. Do I really think there is a problem in Kokomo? Absolutely! I will tell you why. In the beginning, when the local story ran and word spread that I was asking questions, the phone calls were from sick retirees and families who had lost loved ones. But later that changed. The calls changed. The calls were now coming from people who had never worked in the factories but were sick with rare cancers and leukemia's. Some of them children. You might be thinking, "Okay, so people get cancer," but this was different. The calls I get come from people who live or have lived in areas that correlate with the areas that the retirees say the dumping occurred.

I got an urgent message one night from the daughter of a woman who lives in a neighborhood on the west side of our town. Her mother had been diagnosed with breast cancer and so had four other women in the neighborhood. This is not likely a coincidence. Another neighborhood on the southeast side has multiple cases of a rare brain tumor, glioblastoma and leukemias.

I found myself paying close attention to these people when they called. This had gone beyond the factories and it had affected our community. I found out quite innocently that covering it up is still part of the solution.

I was participating in a fundraiser one day at a local golf course. I was paired with a nice guy to ride along with on the golf cart. We shared small talk. He told me that he was a project manager for a development company. Soon a lady came around and asked if we'd like some water or drinks. The guy turned to me and said, "I was told when I came to town to work on this project to never drink the water here." Of course my radar went right up.

The day went on and his water changed to beer. I took this as an opportunity to ask about the water. He told me that they had built a whole area of rental homes in town and discovered afterward that there were barrels of chemicals underneath the land they built on. He said, "I have no clue what they are going to do, if anything."

This is what angers and fuels me. These new apartment complexes and housing are built over contaminated ground. It's the same thing these companies did to their employees. They know it's harmful but they also know it takes years of exposure before people start getting sick. We have to hold them accountable for proper clean up. It's important to know the history of your neighborhood and speak up. It can take only one voice.

Now, I'm going to tell you about a woman we will call Nicki. Nicki saw my social media page and reached out to me. Nicki was a single woman, a successful woman, living the American Dream in the sense that she had a great job, owned her own home, a couple dogs, and enjoyed retreating up to her camper on the weekends. Nicki was actually living a nightmare. She had TCE and PCE vapors in her home. She lives in a neighborhood across the street from where Plant 5 stood.

I went to visit her and listen to her story. We walked the neighborhood to the front where her grandma's house once stood. As I was walking I noticed monitoring wells in the streets and sidewalks. She shared with me memories of better days as she spent a lot of her childhood at her grandma's house.

A sign at Plant 5 across from Nicki's neighborhood

She told me about her Aunt who had suffered from a rare, aggressive breast cancer and had also lived in the neighborhood.

We walked back towards her house and she shared with me her own health problems. She had purchased her home 6 years ago. Prior to that she had lived next door with her brother for 7 years. She has suffered from severe fatigue, migraines, and multiple miscarriages. "This is why I don't have kids." She has made frequent trips to the doctors who, despite testing, can't find a reason for miscarriages or other ailments.

The EPA finally admitted in 2017, after testing, that Nicki had TCE and PCE vapors in her home along with some of her other neighbors. A lot of the houses in this area are owned by landlords who rent them out and refused testing. It would take another two years before Nicki would get a mitigation system installed and she still has yet to get final results of the number of PCEs and TCEs detected in her home. She can't sell her home with this cloud hanging over it. She's responsible for the cost of maintaining the mitigation system. Her cellar floor was covered with plastic and she was told that would take care of it.

Really? Is that their answer to everything? Just cover it up and hope no one gets sick? This site is currently under federal cleanup with no mention of the neighborhoods surrounding it. Nicki has been the only one brave enough to speak up. I see you, Nicki. I don't have an answer yet but I'm fighting for you and with you.

How many Nickis are in our town? Some who don't know and some who know but are afraid to speak up.

PCE And TCE

We've all heard about PCE and TCE at some point or another in regards to the environment. I was like most people. I had heard about them in the news but never gave much thought until I started investigating locally in my hometown. The effects of exposure to any chemical depend on a variety of factors...

- When you are exposed (during pregnancy, in infancy, etc.)
- How much you are exposed to
- How long you are exposed

- How you are exposed (breathing, drinking), and

- What your personal traits and habits are.

Because of these variables, not everyone who is exposed to trichloroethylene (TCE), tetrachloroethylene (PCE), benzene, or vinyl chloride exposure will develop a health problem.

Here's a list of health effects with sufficient evidence for causation from TCE... (See page 79 for sources.)

- Kidney cancer

- Non-Hodgkin lymphoma

- Cardiac defects

Bladder cancer is a health effects with sufficient evidence for causation from PCE.

Here's a list of health effects with sufficient evidence for causation from benzene:

- Leukemias

- Non-Hodgkin lymphoma

Liver cancer is a health concern with sufficient evidence for causation from vinyl chloride.

Health effects with positive findings in at least one study that evaluated exposure to TCE and/or PCE...

- Chonal atresia (nasal passages blocked with bone or tissue)

- Eye defects

- Low birth weight

- Fetal death

- Major malformations

- Miscarriage

- Neural tube defects

- Oral cleft defects (including cleft lip)

- Small for gestational age

- Breast cancer

- Cervical cancer

- Esophageal cancer

- Lung cancer

- Hodgkins disease

- Ovarian cancer

- Prostate cancer

- Rectal cancer

- Impaired immune system function

- Neurological effects (delayed reaction times, problems with short-term memory, visual perception, attention, and color vision)

- Neurobehavioral performance deficits (delayed recall and deficits in visual perception), decreased blink reflex, and mood effects (confusion, depression and tension)

- Severe, generalized hypersensitivity skin disorder (an autoimmune-related disease)

Health effects with positive findings in at least one study that evaluated exposure to benzene:

- Aplastic anemia

- Myelodysplastic syndromes

- Miscarriage

Health effects with positive findings in at least one study that evaluated exposure to vinyl chloride:

- Brain cancer (20)

- Lung cancer (21)

- Soft tissue cancer (20)

- Liver cirrhosis (22)

These links between exposure and health are based on studies with positive associations between exposures to these chemicals and development of health effects. This is why it is so important to be aware of your surroundings and your neighborhoods.

CHAPTER 9

I'M A CANCER SURVIVOR

My Own Cancer Diagnosis

I was diagnosed with lung cancer in the fall of 2015. I had a large 12x8 cm tumor on my left lung. Fortunately, it had not spread and it was mostly necrotic. It took the surgeon seven samples during a lung biopsy before any live cancer cells could be detected.

Yes, I was a smoker and my first thought was I did this to myself. At the time of diagnosis, environmental factors never entered my mind except for the kind of my own doing, even though I was in the thick of following up on stories of illegal dumping and factory contamination all over town. I thought, "I'm a smoker and it caught up with me." My team of doctors did find it odd that I was only 49. It's not that common. But, my focus was on me and getting well. I would own my bad habit.

Before I share my testimony below, I want to fast forward to the fall of 2019. I had met Debbie Corcoran through a mutual friend. Debbie was a lot like me. Debbie's daughter had been diagnosed with a rare environmentally-related cancer. Debbie was on a mission to find out who was responsible and how to get it cleaned up.

Debbie is from a small Indiana town about 2 hours away. She and I spent hours and late nights on the phone digging through IDEM and EPA files. These files about contamination are public, but you have to know how to navigate them. IDEM and EPA do not make it easy, probably because they are fulfilling their lawful duty by publishing them, but yet don't want the general public knowing what might be under their neighborhood, so it's not easy to navigate and it takes hours.

To clarify, IDEM is who regulates environmental issues for Indiana. Debbie taught me how to get into these files. One night I had a yearly check-up coming up. We were talking about that and the usual "scanxiety," as cancer patients refer to it. Debbie said, "Didn't you say you worked downtown?" I could here Debbie typing away for what seemed like hours and then there was silence. Finally she said, "Oh girl," and then directed me on my end to the files she found. My job downtown started when I was 22 and lasted until I was 47. I had worked 25 years in an office building on top of and next to a huge toxic soup of chemicals. Benzene, trichloroethylene, hexavalent chromium, asbestoes and the list goes on. Chemicals I had become all to familiar with. The office has been closed several years now. It was a small business with a small group of employees, but it hit me like a smack in the face.

One employee had passed from Non Hodgkins Lymphoma, one from lung cancer, another from esophageal cancer, one from pancreatic cancer and two from severe COPD. There were 10 employees and these diagnoses came in a span of 10 years. Then there was me and my diagnosis. After that I started researching the neighborhood I grew up in and found out there were 4 lung cancer diagnoses in the neighborhood I grew up in, including mine. Two of them younger than me at diagnosis and one of them being 19 years old.

I am not looking for a place to lay blame for my own diagnosis, but to raise awareness for folks and encourage people to know your neighborhood, know where you work, ask questions, and research. There has always been a stigma with lung cancer but lung cancer is on the rise among non-smokers. Don't always assume it's smoking. The evidence I uncovered about my own work history has me asking, was it the smoking, the chemicals, or a combination? I remember my first day on the job and our sales manager said to me, "Mrs. Roe, don't drink out of the water fountain." I can't begin to tell you how many times I tell people, "don't drink the water."

My Testimony

I accepted Jesus as my Savior many years ago as a young girl. I have a good friend who has gently prodded me to give my testimony.

Here it is, the good news. Jesus will not only save you, but he will meet you wherever you are.

During a hot hot summer in 2015, I had a patient without family who lived all alone with a houseful of cats. I tried to show her love by doing extra for her, beyond my traditional job. One day she asked me to shampoo her carpets, which were covered in cat hair. The heat index was 105 that day, but I did it anyway.

As I emptied the machine, which was caked with hair and grime, I started to cough and my eyes started to water and it didn't stop. For a month I coughed and sneezed and blamed it on allergies. I went to the doctor over and over, but found no relief. Finally, a nurse practitioner sent me to the hospital for a chest X-ray to rule out pneumonia.

I waited until I was done seeing patients on Friday, ran to the hospital for an X-ray and went back to the office to finish up so I could start my vacation. My siblings were coming to my house to celebrate our brother Rick's retirement. My phone rang at the office. It was a nurse, and she said indelicately, "Get back to the hospital! You have a huge mass in your left lung."

A terrifying fear set in. No one in my family was available by phone. Jim, my husband, was on a flight back from work. My sister was on flight coming to Indiana. The office staff had gone home for the day. I went back to the hospital for a CT scan and made the radiation tech promise to have the nurse practitioner call me that night. No way was I waiting til Monday for the results.

She called at 7:55, and I remember every word she said. "I'm only 25. I've never had to do this before," she said. "Can we pray first?"

She prayed for my peace and healing and then read the report. I had a 12x8 cm mass in my left lung with characteristics of malignancy.

As soon as I hung up the phone, I emailed Dr. Moore, who had taken care of my dad years before. "It's Sherry," I wrote. "I'm in trouble. Call me."

And she did. Five minutes later, she called and promised to have my records couriered to her house. I will call you Monday morning at 8 am with a plan. Try not to worry, Sherry."

I work in hospice, so of course I worried all weekend. I was terrified. My first thoughts were for my children. I felt like history was repeating itself. I decided then and there I wouldn't tell them until I knew my prognosis.

Next I told my sister Glenda, who has been my mom longer than she has been my sister. She has bossed me around and looked out for me my whole life. She said, sternly, "Everything will be okay. Right now we are going to focus on Rick's life achievement. We will deal with cancer on Monday."

We expected 100 people for Rick's party, so we decided right then that we were going to get prepped for the party and tell the rest of my family on Sunday morning before they headed back home. The business of preparing for the party would help keep my fear at bay.

Next I called my supervisor. I told her that she could tell the staff and to have them pray for me, but not to post anything on social media. I was going to be spending a lot of time at home, and I wanted one place that was normal.

True to her word, Dr. Moore called me Monday morning with a schedule of labs, pet scan, biopsy, etc. That Friday she called with good news. Though the mass was large, it hadn't spread. She said, "I can cure you. Be at my office at 9 am Monday. We will hook you up to some poison and kill some cancer."

I went to bed that night and stayed there until Sunday afternoon, when Jim threw back the covers and said, "Get your ass up. You aren't special. Just like the rest of us, you don't get to know how or when you are going to die."

I was fortunate that I was otherwise healthy at 49, according to Dr. Moore and my health team. As they said, "You can withstand having everything, including the kitchen sink, thrown at you and that is our intention." The symptoms I was having were indeed from allergies. I never had traditional lung cancer symptoms, no weight loss, no shortness of breath. The plan was 4 rounds of chemo with two different cocktails and 33 concurrent radiation treatments. I cut my hair short and kept my circle small.

I reached out to Bridgett Siter and Marla Geiger, two of the most godly women I knew. I asked them to keep it private and pray. They've prayed me through treatment and each and every scan. I had it in my mind that they had a better in with Jesus than me because, well, I'm notorious for my potty mouth.

Then there is Ruby, a co-worker and a good friend. Every morning before we started our work day, Ruby and I would talk at 5:00. She was one of the first people I called when I got the news. The phone calls continued every morning, and quite frankly, I depended on them because Ruby could say anything she wanted and she knew what I needed. Sometimes I needed an ass-chewing.

When you work at Guardian Angel Hospice, you become part of a unique family. Hospice is a ministry, and we are often referred to as the angels. The owners and my co-workers donated their vacation hours when mine ran out to make sure I still received my paycheck. I had more than 100 angels praying over me daily. I received texts and calls daily of prayer, uplifting words, and offers of support from all the angels.

Ocean is our director of volunteers who wears many hats. When there is a need among our staff or in the community, she shows up in a big way. She organized a meal train with all the other angels to have a hot meal delivered to my family every day while I was going through treatment and recovering. Kathy, our nurse practitioner and my sister-in-law, paid my health insurance premium while I was off work. Tammy worked in the call center. She and her husband also have a popular haunted house every year called Edge of Insanity. They donate their proceeds to charities and to families in need. That year they chose my family.

Even though I chose to keep my circle small, I had a tremendous support system and that is so vital when you are faced with something like this. Jim was my constant cheerleader. He kept me out of the bed and moving. He sat with me at treatments and sat beside me afterwards until I would come back around after the third day.

Lexy, a daughter, went through her senior year, going to classes half day, and working 40 hours a week. Lexy and Soph, another daughter, did all the housework and ran errands for the family.

Jimmy, a son, helped with the laundry and household chores, too. Jax, another son, did all the outside work, and Ryder, also a son, kept me company and gave the best foot rubs.

I had my last treatment on January 2, 2016, and was released to go back to work 4 weeks later. The first weekend call I was sent to was about 2 hours away; a stage 4 lung cancer patient. One of my co-workers had to talk me all the way there, constantly reminding me that it wasn't my story. That was a turning point for me mentally towards healing. I knew I was doing what I was supposed to be doing.

Then I learned what scanxiety was. The first scan was 3 months after the end of my treatments. That was a big one; it showed remission. I had a scan every 3 months the first two years. It was like I was living my life in quarters. In 2018, I went to every 6 months. That was better, but I was a hot mess for weeks before each scan. And I was relieved after each. The results were good.

During that time, I worked with a nurse named Sara. She was a good friend to me and so patient! When you've had cancer, you question every symptom. I would call Sara in the morning, and she would say, "Roe, what kind of cancer do you have today?" God Bless her, she has became a forever sister and has talked me down more times than I could ever count.

In the fall of 2018, I was still in remission and Dr. Moore said, "I will see you in a year." A whole year without scanxiety! Was the chance of recurrence in the back of my mind? Absolutely!

I paid off the last of my chemo bills just before my annual scan in August of 2019. This time I wasn't nervous when she said the results were good and she'd see me in a year.

I had another big step mentally that year. I was sitting in Ocean's office. It was a Friday and my last day before vacation. I said, I'm coming back in Monday morning to do my paperwork. She didn't understand so I confessed to her that ever since that "scary" phone call that I never do paperwork on a Friday anymore. We went on talking for a few minutes and I got up to leave and I said, "I'm headed out." Ocean said, "No you aren't, you are going to go do your paperwork first." Anybody that knows Ocean, knows you don't tell her No, you just do what she says.

As ridiculous and insignificant as it sounds, it was a huge mental well-being step for me and I'm forever grateful that Ocean recognized my fear and gave me that push.

Dr. Moore gave me three rules when I started this journey. She said, "Never look at the internet or statistics because they are outdated and don't apply to your situation. Don't listen to medical advice about your cancer from others unless they have an oncology degree. And surround yourself with positive people."

I remember a well-meaning but ignorant person once said to me, "Hey you only have a 14% survival rate. I know because I read it on the internet." That thought was in the back of my mind as I approached my 5 year scans.

Let me tell you about our Jesus. He doesn't look at statistics either! He doesn't have an oncology degree, but he is the Great Physician and Healer, and I believe he had a hand in all this, from the day I shampooed the carpets. I believe he was with Dr. Moore, Dr. Price, and Dr. Salter when they sat down to plan a treatment protocol that would work for me.

Cancer has been a blessing to me. Let me tell you why. The sky is a more brilliant blue now. The colors of the leaves are more vibrant. Daily tasks are not annoying anymore; I do them with love. Being the hands and feet of Jesus is close to my heart. It has made me much better at my job. I don't tolerate mean people, but I do give more grace. And my potty mouth - it's still there but I'm a work in progress. I'm a sinner but a Believer, because Jesus met me right where I was and showed me he is still Jesus.

In 2020, I waited anxiously for Dr. Moore to come in the room and talk with me about my 5 year scans. She sat down at her computer, turned around and smiled and said, "Sherry, go live your life. You are an official survivor now. You are cured!

By his stripes, I am healed.

CHAPTER 10

ONE DAY

For Tony

My oldest brother Tony passed away on August 20, 2019. His death was sudden and unexpected and left our hearts even more broken. Tony was an artist. He went to IU on an art scholarship after high school. He ended up in Zainesville, Ohio, a town on the Ohio river where he built a life and legacy of his art. He painted murals around downtown and in parks. One of his pieces was adopted as a logo for a big oil company.

Tony was a big supporter of the arts in his hometown and it was always a dream of his to have his work displayed for the public to see in a gallery show. Carolyn, his widow, made this happen last year as all of his pieces were on display in a showing at the Zainesville Appalachian Art Project in Ohio. All of his pieces but one that is. My sister, Glenda, was going through some old boxes and found a piece titled "One Day." I saw it and immediately thought to myself, "this has to be the cover of this book." The three stars symbolize mom, dad, and Tony. Perhaps this piece was tucked away for a reason, for display for this very story.

Tony's story is important because the death of our parents was a greater loss to Tony than the rest of us. It may have been even more for him to carry than we realized.

Tony was six months old when our parents married. Mom had gotten pregnant with Tony and married his biological father, Junior. When the marriage didn't work out, Mom was left a single mom in the 50s. Dad and Junior were good friends. Dad stepped in to help young Thelma and Tony. When Dad shipped off to serve, he and Thelma corresponded by letters while he was overseas. Dad came home and started courting her and they were soon married when he came back from service. Junior relinquished his parental rights, and Dad adopted Tony as an infant. Tony told me once that he was around 8 years old at the bowling alley and this nice man gave him some money to play arcade games. That was Junior, but he didn't know it.

Junior had settled down and gone on to raise a family with his new wife, Ronda. Our families were often together as they shared the same group of friends. As a child, I would often stay at their house, especially when my mom was sick in the hospital. Ronda was very kind to me, and she was a good cook. Tony had been told that Dad adopted him, but he was about 35 before he learned the truth about who his biological father was. Tony had four other siblings. Though Ronda encouraged the relationship, Junior said he had an agreement with our mom that he'd stay out of Tony's life. That made me sad. I don't know what Mom's reasoning was, but this man was trying to honor it.

As I became a young woman, I developed a relationship with Ronda. She was one of the most genuine Christian women I had ever met. This other family was much like our's, so it was not surprising that we had mutual friends. I never tired of hearing Ronda tell me the story of the day my mom died and Junior told her to cook a pot of green beans and take them over to Jerry and his kids. She said, "It felt so weird, but it wasn't."

I remember those green beans, I had them plenty of times when I stayed at their home. I knew what she meant about it being weird when it wasn't. As an adult, looking back, I thought how awkward it must have been to have me at her house, looking out for me while my mom was sick. Knowing Ronda as I had come to know her, it wasn't weird at all. She was a woman caring for a child who needed a mother's love.

Why is this important? At Dad's funeral as all of us kids stood at the casket, Junior approached us, frail and walking with a cane, Ronda assisting him. They came to show their love and support for Tony and our dad, their lifelong friend.

Tony's biological dad had received the same diagnosis as Dad. He worked at the plant, too. He passed away a few months later. Tony buried both of his dads within a year from the same rare leukemia caused from the chemical benzene.

Ronda continued a relationship with all of the Dukes kids. When I was diagnosed with cancer myself in 2015, she was the first person who stopped by, coming in the door, calling out, "Hey, Sweetheart, I've brought food, so you don't have to cook." The green beans were as good as I remembered and were just as nourishing for my soul as they were my body. It wasn't weird anymore. This is how life and love come full circle. Ronda passed away recently. I had the honor and privilege to help care for her. The day she passed, I thought to myself, I've now buried two mothers.

Continuing the Fight

So remember the young Texas lawyer that won dad over with his rendition of the tune from Andy Griffith? Shortly before dad's case was filed in 2010, Erick left the firm he was at to start his own practice. I learned early on, after dad signed his case, that Erick is the real deal and genuinely cares about his clients' injustices and fighting for them to right those wrongs. Even though he was no longer involved in my dad's case, Erick would text or call me periodically over the years to ask about how the family was and we would exchange small talk. In 2015, as I realized the magnitude of contamination in our town, I also realized I was in way over my head. I sat down one evening and called Erick. I told him about all the workers' stories, the cancer rates, and sick people. He listened without interrupting and when I finished he said, "I want you to watch the movie *A Civil Action*, then watch it a second time, and call me back."

The film *A Civil Action* is about the court case of multiple families that have lost their children to leukemia. These families believed that the city's tap water was contaminated with trichloroethylene which ultimately led to these children's untimely death. It's based on a true story.

Before we hung up, he said, "I believe you're onto something. I'm asking you to watch this not to discourage you, but so you know the commitment and resilience it takes to follow through."

I watched the movie and, to be honest, I was a little discouraged and more overwhelmed than before I called him. I called him the next week and shared my thoughts. I also told him that I wanted to go forward and help expose these factories and bring public awareness to the contamination in our town. I was already an amateur activist, but I hung up the phone that day as an environmental investigator.

You might wonder what an environmental investigator does. Well, I do exactly what I did for my dad's case. I chase down co-workers and records and get the goods on these corporate bastards to help bring justice to these families. I continue to work towards the big picture.

Currently I have been working with some other activists and researchers in a small southern Indiana town that is overcome with cancer clusters from multiple plumes, tainted water and, yes, cover up that goes back years. I am a member of their community action board so I can observe, learn, help and bring that knowledge back to our town. These researchers are testing the air in homes, soil, and water wells. There are lots of sick children in this town. I see the desperation in the eyes of their parents, some with children fighting rare cancers and those who have lost children. It's not about money. It's about wanting someone to pay. The goal is to start a community action board here locally in my town. The researchers want to come here and test the air in homes in suspicious areas.

Do I think there is a problem here in Kokomo? Absolutely. Vapor intrusion occurs when old buried chemicals leak into the ground and water. It gets in our wells and aquifers. It then can seep into cracks in homes and thus the air we breathe. This testing is important in proving the need for cleanup and getting the EPA involved. The stories of dumping that the retirees have told me about and the locations coincide with the people who are sick and where they live. We call these "stories" a lot, but they are factual reports from eyewitness accounts.

In the meantime, I freelance as an investigator. I work with Erick on cases here locally and in southern Indiana. I get to know these people and their stories that I carry home in my heart. It fuels me to work harder to expose these companies and their cover-ups. I get discouraged and overwhelmed pouring over old records late at night and when I do I get a cup of coffee and turn on *A Civil Action*. I encourage you to watch it. The good guys win in the end and one day we will win against these injustices committed against our loved ones and the towns we live in.

I have the commitment and resilience to continue this fight for the sacrifices that my parents made for me and ultimately paid with their life for their loyalty to their job. My sometimes unique way of getting this information prompted a phone call from a firm in New York in the summer of 2019. The attorney said, "I represent the widow of a painter who worked at a GM plant in New York and succumbed to AML." This was the same Leukemia my dad had. She went onto say, "You are becoming well known amongst attorneys all over the US for your ability to get the discovery done. You are an Erin Brockovich of sorts. We'd like to retain your services as an investigator in this case." I don't tell that story to boast but because it was a defining moment when I knew that I was making a difference for these factory workers and their families. I am honoring my parents with my work.

Some days I relate my life to Erin Brockovich. Although I work in hospice during the day, late nights are often spent going through case files. Days off are sometimes spent on the road from early morning until late at night talking with families, taking work and health histories, listening to stories of their loved ones who are sick or have passed. Erick and I will tell them the story of how we met at the beginning of my dad's case and how we came to work together. Their stories are imprinted in my heart and just like the real Erin, I can recite each person and their story by heart. I tell them about mom and dad. I share their tears.

I am reminded, too, how life has come full circle by the career paths I have chosen. I followed my heart to work in hospice after my dad's death because it is truly a ministry. I work as an environmental investigator for the same attorney that signed my dad's case so long ago. I never doubt that we cross paths with people for a reason and while we may not know why at that moment, it will be revealed in time.

These corporations don't like to admit wrong-doing, but my work is helping to make sure some of their profits go back to the people and one day hold these companies accountable for putting their profits over people.

HISTORY OF DELCO IN KOKOMO, INDIANA

1935 – The Crosley Radio Corporation starts building Chevrolet radios at the former Haynes Automobile plant site, after the Kokomo Chamber of Commerce gives Crosley the building free of charge.

1936 – General Motors buys Crosly and launches the Delco Radio Division, with 428 employees in the plant.

1937 – A second plant is built south of Plant 1 to manufacture carburetors.

1940 – Delco Radio produced its millionth car radio.

1941 – Delco Radio ends most civilian production and focuses on producing anti radar devices and military radio equipment in support of the war effort.

1943 – Plant 3 is built east of Plant 2 to build two-way radios for the war effort.

1948 – A new plant is built southeast of Plant 1 for final assembly operations.

1951 – A new plant is built on North Washington Street to build car radios as well as meet the increasing demand for military production.

1952 – Delco Radio produced its 10 millionth car radio, and production of circuit boards begins.

1954 – An administrative building goes up on Firmin Street, and a large manufacturing area is built southeast of Plant 2.

1961 – Three plants are built on U.S. 31. Delco produces it's 30 millionth car radio.

1962 – Began integrated circuit development program.

1964 – Plant 9 is built at the U.S. 31 complex.

1965 – Delco produces its first car stereo.

1968 – Delco Radio produces its 50 millionth radio.

1970 – The Milwaukee AC Electronics Division is consolidated with Delco Radio and renamed the Delco Electronics Division. Products include guidance and navigation systems for Apollo space flights.

1975 – Delco establishes the Solid State Design Center in Kokomo.

1981 – Delco produces its 200 millionth speaker.

1982 – The company announces a major expansion program in Kokomo that includes construction of a 65,000 square foot "clean room" for manufacturing semiconductor chips.

1985 – Delco Electronics achieved corporate status when it's named a subsidiary of the newly formed GM Hughes Electronic Corporation.

1987 – The Corporate Technology Center opens.

1988 – The company introduces a heads-up display for cars.

1992 – All GMHE automotive electronics development activities are integrated into the Delco Electronics Corporation.

1997 – Delco Electronics moves from Hughes Electronics to Delphi Automotive Systems, where it is renamed Delphi Delco Electronics Systems.

1999 – General Motors is spun off Delphi Automotive Systems as a separate, publicly-traded company.

2002 – Delphi Automotive Systems becomes the Delphi Corporation in order to reflect all of its products and services.

2005 – Delphi declares Chapter 11 bankruptcy.

Delco Electronics was a wholly-owned subsidiary-based company owned by General Motors and based in Kokomo, a factory town 60 miles due north of Indianapolis on the old Highway 31, before the bypass was completed in 1952.

In Stoplight City (Kokomo), the US 31 plant spans 3.9 million square feet.

Kokomo's population has fluctuated with the rise and fall of the automotive and steel industries, with a current population of roughly 46,000. At its peak in the 1970s, Delco employed nearly 30,000 people.

Plants 1, 2, 3 and 6 have been subject to a federally-ordered clean up. Most recently, Plant 5 was added to the Superfund Federal Cleanup List.

In 1993, newly appointed CEO Gary Dickinson referred to the company as "a 500 pound gorilla." (Beck, Bill "More than car radios" The Free Library 01 November, 1993)

SOURCES

Massachusetts Department of Public Health, Centers for Disease Control and Prevention, Massachusetts Health Research Institute. 1996. Final report of the *Woburn environmental and birth study*. Boston, Massachusetts: Massachusetts Department of Public Health.

Bove F, Shim Y, Zeitz P. 2002. *Drinking water contaminants and adverse pregnancy outcomes: a Review*. Environ Health Perspect 110(S): 61-73.

Bove FJ, Fulcomer MC, Klotz JB, Esmart J, et al. 1995. *Public drinking water contamination and birth outcomes*. Am J Epidemiol 141:850-62.

Rodenbeck SE, Sanderson LM, Rene A. 2000. *Maternal exposure to trichloroethylene in drinking water and birthweight outcomes*. Arch Environ Health 55:188–194.

Khattak S, K-Moghtader G, McMartin K, Barrera M, et al. 1999. *Pregnancy outcome following gestational exposure to organic solvents: a prospective controlled study*. JAMA 281(12): 1106-09.

Pesticide and Environmental Toxicology Section, Office of Environmental Health Hazard Assessment, California Environmental Protection Agency. 1999. *Public health goal for trichloroethylene in drinking water*. Sacramento, California.

Pesticide and Environmental Toxicology Section, Office of Environmental Health Hazard Assessment, California Environmental Protection Agency. 2001. *Public health goal for tetrachloroethylene in drinking water.* Sacramento, California.

Aschengrau A, Rogers S, Ozonoff D. 2003. *Perchloroethylene-contaminated drinking water and the risk of breast cancer: additional results from Cape Cod, Massachusetts, USA.* Environ Health Perspect 111(2):167-73.

Wartenberg D, Reyner D, Scott CS. 2000. *Trichloroethylene and cancer: epidemiologic evidence.* Environ Health Perspect 108(S2):161-176.

National Toxicology Program (NTP). *Report on carcinogens.* 14th edition. Research Triangle Park, NC: US Department of Health and Human Services; 2016.

Mundt KA, Birk T, Burch MT. 2003. *Critical review of the epidemiological literature on occupational exposure to perchloroethylene and cancer.* Int Arch Occup Environ Health. 76:473-91.

Paulu C, Aschengrau A, Ozonoff D. 1999. *Tetrachloroethylene-contaminated drinking water in Massachusetts and the risk of colon-rectum, lung, and other cancers.* Environ Health Perspect 107(4):265-71.

Chiu WA, Jinot J, Scott CS, Makris SL et al. 2013. *Human health effects of trichloroethylene: key findings and scientific issues.* Environ Health Perspect 121:303-311.

Reif JS, Burch JB, Nuckols JR, Metzgar L, et al. 2003. *Neurobehavioral effects of exposure to trichloroethylene through a municipal water supply.* Environ Res 93:248-258

Sources

Feldman RG, Chirico-Post J, Proctor SP. 1988. *Blink reflex latency after exposure to trichloroethylene in well water.* Environ Health 43: 143-148.

Cooper GS, Makris SL, Nietert PJ, Jinot J. 2009. *Evidence of Autoimmune-Related Effects of Trichloroethylene Exposure from Studies in Mice and Humans.* Environ Health Perspect 117:696–702.

Khan HA. 2007. Short Review: *Benzene's toxicity: a consolidated short review of human and animal studies.* Hum Exp Toxicol. 26; 677-685.

IARC *Monographs on the Evaluation of Carcinogenic Risks to Humans,* Vol 97: 1,3-Butadiene, Ethylene Oxide and Vinyl Halides (Vinyl Fluoride, Vinyl Chloride and Vinyl Bromide). Lyon, France 2008.

Bofetta P, Matisane L, Mundt KA, Dell LD. 2003. *Meta-analysis of studies of occupational exposure to vinyl chloride in relation to cancer mortality.* Scand J Work Environ Health. 29:220-229.

Scelo G, Constantinescu V, Csiki I, Zaridze D, et al. 2004. *Occupational exposure to vinyl chloride, acrylonitrile and styrene and lung cancer risk (Europe). Cancer Causes Control.* 15:445-452.

Grosse Y, Baan R, Straif K, Secretan B, et al. 2007. *Carcinogenicity of 1,3-butadiene, ethylene oxide, vinyl chloride, vinyl fluoride, and vinyl bromide. Oncology: The Lancet.* 8:679-680.

ABOUT THE AUTHOR

Sherry Roe spends her days working in hospice, caring for and ensuring the comfort and quality of life for her patients during their time left on earth. She spends her spare time as an environmental investigator, conducting interviews and uncovering years old corporate corruption and contamination to help ensure the communities that you and I live in are safe and free from contamination.

Sherry lives in Kokomo, Indiana with her husband, Jim. They have raised five children and are enjoying their first grandchild. If you would like to know more about Sherry's work, you can follow her Facebook page; Profits Over People.

NOTES

NOTES

Made in the USA
Middletown, DE
06 October 2022

12088122R00049